FINAL DEMANDS

FINAL DEMANDS

PETER READING

Secker & Warburg
POETRY

First published in England 1988 by
Martin Secker & Warburg Limited
54 Poland Street, London W1V 3DF

Copyright © Peter Reading 1988

British Library Cataloguing in Publication Data
Reading, Peter
 Final demands.
 I. Title
 821'.914   PR6068.E27

ISBN 0-436-40993-3

Printed in Great Britain by
Biddles Ltd, Guildford and King's Lynn

[Clearing the family's papers for next crowd's vacant possession:
brown leaves of letters whose dead still correspond with ourselves.]

[Chucked in the Parkray, naff juvenilia…]
$P_2 O_5$ *drip-fed from a lead pipette*
  fails to restore dull cotyledons
    Liquinured past revivification

[Anhydrous *lauriers*. Stubbornly unrevivable old leaves.
  Drying up/not drying out.] —— ◡ ◡ | —— ◡ ◡ | ——

Crapulous death-fright at 3 in the morning,
                              grim fantasizing…
Morphean, painless, idyllic expiry, easeful, Sabaean…
duvet and pillow-case metamorphose to sweet-smelling
                              sered leaves,
thick-fallen under two olive boles grafted, canopied tightly,
such as the storm-wrecked Laertides, life-wracked,
                              sunk in exhausted
snug at the end of Book V… and a phial of bland analgesics
(comforting rattle) and, fumous, a single-vintage Madeira,
buttery caramel fatty, the cobwebbed bottle of Bual
stencilled COLHEITA 1915 in white relief paint runes…

dreamingly crawls and his hands have now raked a
                              litter together,
spacious and deep, for the leafage is lying in plentiful
                              downfall,
lays him to rest in the midst of the leaves and
                              piles them around him,
just as a man might cover a brand with char-blacked ashes,
guarding the seed of the fire for his tribe to use in the future,
so does he deeply immerse in the fall of past generations,
litter of leaves, not from olives, but the sepia, brittle
leaves of the letters of lost correspondents, infinite,
                              death-frail
  (Croxley, papyrus and bond), sinks in the lines of the dead.

Clutching a chicken's furcula, festively,
[dull throb in slightly purpled first knuckle joint]
   curling the left hand little finger
      tight round the bifurcate, child-tugged fusion –

[twinge of it yesterday also as you played chess with the
                                        nipper...
  premature arthritis? cramp?] wish: *may they not miss me*
                                          much.

CHAPTER THE LAST

Tethered by long ropes to iron pins spiked in the sphagnum, some half-dozen skewbald ponies had been snatching at tufts of the coarse grass sprouting between gorse and ling on the Common where a gaily-painted waggon and grey-green thick canvas beehive-shaped tent betokened the eerie presence of "Mosey" the gipsy and his little tribe.

She and Mary had become aware, as they emerged from the brake, of the sweet scent of wood-smoke. An old woman attended the fire, above which swung, from an ingenious arrangement of stout sticks, a capacious char-crusted kettle, wherefrom was effused the aromatic distillation of some savoury mess redolent of garlic and wild fowls.

Upon some nearby low gnarled May bushes, richly clotted with their dollops of new curdy blossoms, hung, or rather were pierced by the sharp thorns, items of bright-hued Romany attire, freshly laundered and arrayed thus to dry, looking like nothing so much as gaudy red, green and blue parakeets perched fluttering.

Somewhat shyly had the sisters advanced, when, looking up from her culinary preoccupations, old Dalleritha, for it was none other than she, apprehended the pair and greeted them cordially enough.

After the crone's prolix wheedling preamble, so characteristic of vulgar intercourse, Emily had explained the philanthropic nature of the sisters' visit. Greedily ogling the medicinal wine reposing in Sophia's straw basket, the beldam had inadvertently run her drooling tongue in one direction across her upper lip and then back the contrary way — a bead of saliva dependant from the corner of her toothless, corrupt maw.

"I s'll be a takin' of that there in for th'old un, lady, indeed to be a savin' of yous the trouble, see?"

But Sophia had been resolute. "No, indeed, good Mistress, for it is no imposition on my dear sister and me, and we have ventured so far from the village that it would seem a task uncompleted were we to return home without having personally seen, and enquired the health of, old Mr Moses."

Grudgingly then, and with many a mumbled, scarcely comprehensible complaint, had the ancient materfamilias led the way to the tent of her espoused.

At the portal, rough-hewn from a forked bough of hawthorn to make an A-shaped entrance, hung a wicker cage incarcerating a brace of Woodcocks, live, with steep foreheads, large eyes and plumage all straked like dead leaves; poor hapless creatures, destined, it was little to be doubted, for the black kettle. Hard by, upon the turf, lay an old fiddle, so refulgent in the morning sunlight that its varnished curvature gleamed like burnished amber.

When the rough sacking, which served as a door, was lifted aside, there was revealed, as on their earlier visit, the seated Gipsy Moses, enthroned like a Turkish Pasha, sucking at a pungent-smelling stained clay pipe and tracing the strange symbols with charcoal upon the same sheets of skin or coarse paper.

The old man's eyes had not strayed from his weird manuscript as the visitors entered. His poor fingers, their joints and knuckles so swollen and empurpled with the arthritis that they gave the appearance of recently dug-up beetroot tubers, laboriously formed the runes which now, more than ever, reminded Emily of some dimly recollected thing.

She had thought that the hieroglyphs were similar to those shewn her by Mr Bancroft at the Horse Shoe Inn, where some skilful mason had incorporated one of the antique "Roony Stanes" from the derelict Priory into the steps of that hostelry's mounting-block. Like those forgotten, or not yet understood, utterances, which one could not help but contemplate as one mounted to the saddle in

Bancroft's courtyard, these scripts seemed half to reveal and half conceal some strange sad mystery.

★ ★ ★ ★

Or was this, perhaps, the nature of all things written? With an impotent sigh, Emily crumpled the sepia-scrivened leaves, and turned abstractedly towards the hearth. At the last moment, however, she paused and considered once more the timeless, anonymous copperplate of her dead relative. She turned from the flames and, as the dark-eyed gipsy had done so many years before, committed the dry leaves to the long box.

[Punctual, these (with a 40th birthday card) proofs are delivered – dust-jacket mug-shot confirms eyebag-puff/jowl-blubber/flab.]

Ave!, impartial Viral Democracy
(heightening all shared vulnerability):
   down-and-out/Duchess; meths bum/MP;
    temp and autocratrix; Tongan/Taffy…

Chief Cop and high-ranking Sky-Pilot rail of Jovian Vengeance
(*H. sap*'s unable to countenance populational thrivings
  where organisms involved harm or compete with itself).

Summit of scared multinational ideological disparates
(desperate governments limply prescribe us inadequate
                       Johnnies):
  panic-created new pals join in Confederate Fright.

Feb 9/2/44
Horse Shoe Cottage
Breedon

To The Commanding Officer
Dear Sir,
  I being the mother of CH/X104783
Marine Bancroft T. RM Eng
Commond's am writing you regards my
son I should like you to try and do me a
favour if at all possible I am a widow and
I live in house was my late husbands but
he is gone God rest him I should like to
know if my son could be released from
the forces to work in the big estate farm
should you find it possible to do grant me
this favour you could write the Under
Manager Estate Office Tonge and ask
him if work is available for my son so
hoping you will do your best for me I am

sir

 yours faithfull

  Mrs A Bancroft

Everton Boots Rule, Fazzy Fucked Paki Lou,
Quo, Fuck the Pope, Send Black Jungle Bunny Back,
   Mally Cas, Beano, Fuck King Billy,
      Abo-Gaz, Waterloo Skins Rule, Fu Fu.

(Thick rhododendrons and rusted rails ringed the, even then,
                                             disused
open-air bandstand-cum-theatre's crumbling dais, behind which,
stucco, a saucer-like cowl ricocheted a player's performance
– when we were in the IVth we used to trespass there in the
                                             long hols,
strutted the platform *brief candling* it in Thespian piss-take.
   Weeds sprouted from the cracked stage.

                  Weeds overwhelm the wrecked stage.
Urinous, fire-gutted shell in the razed park 26 years on:
pink and fluorescent blue aerosol-written runic sub-lingo…)

Cadder shag Abo-Gaz, Kiddo de Wanker, Death to all Kop Boots,
   L.F.C., Booby Jill SUCKS! Chazza, Fatz Kooly, White Shit.

Trollies marked Kwik Save poke wheels and baskets
                                                    from
thick-frozen slurry massed in the paddle-pool;
    their wires, wind-twanged, zither. Coke cans'
    light alloy clackily rolls on chimed ice,

stuttering, blown, tintinnabulant: —— —— | —— ‿ ‿ | —— ——
—— ‿ ‿ | —— ‿ ‿ | —— || [Bleakly harmonious grot.]

[‘Doesn’t he ever write about *happiness*?’ –
Husband & Wife & Daughter — A Pastoral...]

Thrill of a kite held, twine pulled gust-jerkily
with the slack, tow, taut, tug of a fishing line;
donnée of time and *propre* cartography
    (sunrise in Callow Valley); peaceful
       [mawkish the platitudes], joyful also...

Most savoured plump pork pie ever picnicked-on,
gleaming, the glazed baked crust, like a varnished Strad;
    relish of Meaux tang, crunch-grained; brittle,
peppery, fluted columns of celery;
      hot earthy radishes; crisp frilled lettuce;
bottles of Bass, beck-cold, effervescent gold,
yeasty the foam. Plush cushions of whinberry,
sheep-nibbled, silver-lichened, deep-pillow us...

Paean to celebrate this: [pastoral, cliché, old hat –
blush at the schmaltzy word] Love [but today it
                        is, though, it *is* this].

Tonge, January 12th, 1857.

Dear Emily,

I am very glad to hear that you are well my dear. I wish you a very happy new-year. I have made a song for the church and it has been printed and sung at the school room at Breedon, and Mr Close requested that the children should meet at our house at Tonge on Christmas Eve in order that they might go round Tonge and Breedon to sing Christians Awake and my cards which were printed commencing "God Save our Church & State". Mr Close sent Edwin down with a meat pie of about 14 pound weight, and a Gallon of ale and two large bottles of elderberry wine. There were fifteen altogether that went round. Edwin took his fiddle and Ambrose the flutes, Will Beeton and William Adcock took their Violins. They got three and twenty shillings and sixpence. Your dear little brother Abraham stood on the dining table at Mr Bostock's and got 10d more than the rest. I have been to spend an evening with Mrs Charlton. She was very glad to see me and sent your Grandmother some apples and mince pie. I went for tea to Mrs Ashes of Breedon — Miss Ashes gave me a pretty mat, Mr Joyce gave me a new book to write poetry in, Anne gave me a beautiful drawing of her own.

Ambrose has been very poorly this week but is now rather better. Your Grandmother too has been much weaker of late, she is unaccountably pleased with your letter — she would have it in her possession and said she would have it printed. So pleased to think that you would come in May, (if all be well) to see us. Heppy Joyce came one day, but she went back the same night — she gave her best love to you. Dear Emily have you heard that Mr George Dexter of London died the week before last? I think you have not or you would have said some thing about it. My cousin John Dexter received a letter last week that he was buried on New-years day — I am exceedingly sorry as it was a great consolation for me to think that you had a relation so near at hand, for I had a very high esteem for my dear cousin George Dexter — who, I believe, was a very good man, by the grace of God, especially of late. Poor Mrs Dexter — I wish I could see her to grieve with her. Mr Bancroft at the Horse Shoe Inn, Breedon, is dead and was buried on New-years day and poor Mrs Bancroft is also very poorly. I have not seen any of Mr Bostock's family to speak to them very lately, only at church. I have taken Miss Eliza a bunch of snow-drops this new year and wished her the compliments of the Season. That is all. May God bless you my dear Emily, and grant that you may spend the next year better than you have ever spent one in your life, and that we all may is your dear Mother's wishful prayer. Little Bunting often talks and cries about your being gone, but is so very much pleased with thinking of your coming in May — I hope nothing will happen to prevent it. Send a letter as soon as convenient to let us know how you are going on and if you are well in the midst of the grime and high buildings of the Metropolis. Every one of the family sends his love, Dear Emily, and I have more poetry for you. I am glad to hear that you have prayers every night. Here is The Song.

God save our Church and State
Keep them inviolate
   'Stablished and pure,
From all false doctrines free
And Papal heresy
We as a Nation Pray
   Keep us secure.

Britons once more strike home
Tell the pround Church of Rome
   That we despise
All her idolatries
Masses and mummeries,
And pray that she may fall
   Never to rise.

Season of dangerous nincompoops daubing cul-de-sac stark walls
  prettily bright tangerine: MURDER THE FUCKING SHITE
                                                    POPE.

25 yards away, there is a bleak brick aerosolled dead-end –
  LONG LIVE THE POPE/ORANGE SHIT lividly
                                  sprayed emerald.

(Similar sentiments stimulate crazed trog footy fans' scrawlings –
  LCFC KILL THE REST – baying for mashed flesh and gore.)

Mad, atavistic — REMEMBER SIXTEEN NINETY in orange;
  squirted in green, SMASH THE PRODS. 12th of July, '86:

ludicrous faithfuls in camouflaged shirts and black Balaclavas
  romp in each other's spilt guts; Prods, internecines, RCs...

Season and geography fecund of microcephalic idiots –
  clad in absurd fancy dress, sect, in good faith, *purées* sect.

                    ⎧ gratuitous scrivening
                    ⎨ gratuitous lunacies
  [Strike out the old ⎩ obsessional nastiness.]

Four million
Three ~~hundred~~ years of intractable nitwits' blathersome
                                          humbug,
  [reader, conceive, if you will, a failed solicitor's plaque:

etched into verdigris *Clio & Co., incorporating*
  War-Drum & Tub-Thump & Cant]
                      kneecapping, spatter and splat ⎫
                        poesy, prattle and prate ⎭

Royal Marine Engineer Commando,
Hightown Barracks,
Wrexham,
Denbighshire.

11th February, 1944.

Mrs. A. Bancroft,
Horse Shoe Cottage,
Breedon-on-the-Hill.

Dear Mrs Bancroft,

I regret it is not possible for me to assist in obtaining your son's release from the Forces. It has been laid down by higher authority that neither RM Tradesmen nor ranks of the Special Service Group are eligible for return to civilian occupations.

If any relaxation of these instructions occurs, I will most certainly help.

Yours,

P. Fashpoint-Shellingem (Major RM).

From:
    Major P. Fashpoint-Shellingem
    Royal Marines.
    OC RM Engineer Commando.

Squashed polystyrene Indian Take-Out trays,
eddying grease-smirched chip-papers, Pepsi cans,
  scuttering plastic cups... a *Mirror*'s
    double-page centre-spread, caught in grained wind,

lifts on a gritty, urinous-odoured gust,

  levitates, kite-like, gale-buoyed, higher,

rises in slow flaps, graceful, up-spiralling,

soars to the 19th storey, with pulchritude

slaps against, clingingly hugs

                    one of the uppermost panes.

[Squalor Magnificat, grot, secular ecstasy Hymn,
squall-agitated filth and a high-rise worthy of Paean.]

[Grot is a great democrat. *H. sap* consanguined by waste...
cultural disparates, sub-trog and top prof, Chernobyl/Chelsea
– suddenly neighbourly now: mutual Geigered air croaks.]

Hail, democratic impartiality –
acid rain laced with lethal reactor-leak,
    frozen in pills, percusses, fairly
        riddles the brainpans of vassals/viscounts...

Emerald digits heralding increases
    glow from the charcoaly VDU screens

nineteen floors up where populous feculence
blands, with cathartic distance, to picturesque.
Suddenly, borne on some freak updraught,
    double-page-spread of a *Daily Mirror*

(EFFORTS ARE NOW BEING MADE TO ENCASE THE DAMAGED REACTOR)
    presses against the bright pane,
                        clings, and remains, and remains

Tonge, March 7th, 1857.

My dear Emily,

I did not finish my last letter in consequence of Miss Bowman coming in, and now I bless God in all his goodness and mercy that I am able to write once more. I am like one just risen from death, and I am thinking you had better have a mother with but one breast than to have no mother at all — I know the loss of the best of Mothers.

The country about here has been all on a move respecting me and I cannot think the Queen herself would have had so much real kindness shewn to her. We have visitors every day, and at the first more than we could do with — every one seemed to think it their duty to bring me a present, so that, set it in what light you may, there is infinite mercy attending it. So, I must tell you the wound is healing nicely, but, you may be sure it will not feel as usual — it has grown up partly, and I am thankful the dangerous tumour is removed.

Miss Eliza Bostock attends to me well and has given me a very nice new cloth jacket lined with purple silk and trim'd with beautiful silk braid — she has also given me a dozen of fine Stout from Cox & Malin, a hamper almost as much as a man could carry. Mrs Bostock comes and brings me pots of nice lemon jelly, quart pots — she sent little Joey with 14 new laid eggs and a bottle of Sherry, also broth with Sherry in it and yesterday they sent the Girl with a bird nicely cooked and plenty of gravy. Mrs Curzon sent me Bla-mange and nice mould puddings, Mr J. Bulstrode and Mrs Cross a bottle of good old Sherry, Miss Pegg of Colk a beautiful fowl and eggs, Mr Joyce a fowl, Mrs Joyce a brace of Partridges, Miss Bancroft brought me a basketful of new laid eggs and a large pot of Raspberry-jam, Miss Tompson of our town two bottles of coltsfoot wine, Mr John Joyce a plumb cake, Mrs Mugglestone a large plate of roast veal, Wm. Charlton 2 pots of jam, Lewis a bottle of elder wine, Bessy a bottle of Port, Mrs Eagelfield a part of nice pheasant, Miss Cowlishaw a plate of roast hare & currant jelly, next day light pudding garnished with apricot cheese, Tom a doz Oranges, Thompsons a lot of apples, Fanny a lot of figs, Mr Joyce a bottle of old Port wine, also Mr William half a pint of Brandy, Mr Allan a quart of Port wine, Mr Dawker a fine Woodcock in the feathers all bar'd & bestrak'd as dead leaves of Autumn. But you know there must be such things or I could not have survived the loss of blood and the anguish, and we have been obliged to have folks work here and your Aunts must not want whilst they are sat up with me and attending on me. Sophia had a bed in the corner of the room, while I was extremely bad, but now she sleeps with me again. We have had a leg of mutton or beef every week since I came up stairs — which will soon be 8 weeks. We have had plenty of coal during my illness and the fire up stairs has never been out — we have burnt a cart load, and John sent me some more yesterday. None can behave better to me than they do, God bless them. Write directly.

Yr Loving Mother

[Alcaic (rendered Lounge Bar colloquial):]
Myrsilus dead! Get pissed at the joyous news!...

[(Turbulent content ⎨ formally elegant
                    ⎩ metrically dignified.)
Mad despot captains *still* scuttle ships of state –
    cudgel–thud, steel–clank, shell–zap, gas–sough,
      feculent bilge of the urban ⎨ frontline...]
                                  ⎩ scuppers

Futile pathetic kindly-meant circular:
'We are inviting patients about your age...
    please bring along a urine sample...
        blood pressure tendency... at Health Centre...'

[*What's 40 years here or there on the chrono-stratigraph?*,
                                            you wrote.
    Striking a stance, you were, then;
                            really believe it, though, now.]

[Mostly it's other people's death sentences
one has adopted, striking an attitude;
    suddenly, though...] Among a mess of
        skeleton, puckered skin, part-consumed flesh,

I tug a bifurcate bone with my daughter, win, and, in secret,
    wish *When I rattle my clack, may she not too deeply grieve.*

Lodge Gate House,
Ashbourne Park,
Thorpe.

Dec 21. 44

The C.O. Sir — Is it possible for me to have my
son released from the service on compassionate
grounds? I am a widow now also I have bad health
— periods of arthritis when I need someone in the
home to help me. This prevents me from taking a
situation. I have only my 10/- pension and a small
allotment from my sons pay each week. He is Po.X.
101922 (T) Mne (L/Cpl) B. Hurt Royal Marine
Eng: Commando. He has taken part in the D. Day
assult also the French Coast many times and to
Holland — he now suffers with Sciatica and in
my humble opinion this renders him unfit for the
Commando work. I need him very much here.

Yours Faithfully

Mrs J. Hurt.

[Three-day abdominal pain: dead scared — the liver/the
                                          plonk?
Sudden recovery; with renewed vigour, vivid perception...]

Freezing fog — shivering rooks huddle, wings grizzled with
                                          frost.
Lipstick-smudged fag-end, still fulminant, fizzes steam on a
                                          wet grave.

Loud from a garage a PFSST sternutates in the air-hose.
Bickering Pepsi tins emptily clack on ice-skinned canal top.

Out of an overflow pipe, ice drools, off-white congealed wax.
[Ossless, quotidian; worth, through revived awareness, a paean.]

Under a clay weight dumped on the leather-topped
desk in his study, final demands, accrued
    quarterly/monthly (Access, phone bill,
        water rates, overdraft, life insurance),

flutter in rose-fumed draughts from the garden. [40th
                                        birthday…
    chequebook — the Mrs and kid shan't, at least,
                        be bequeathed debt.]

Lodge Gate House,
Ashbourne Park,
Thorpe.

Jan 1. 45

Sir — A short time ago I wrote you requesting the
release of my son from the service. I now realise
how very mistaken I was in doing this and of
perhaps giving you the impression that he had
failed to help me. I assure you sir that this is not
so, and that every week I have had adequite
assistance from him. He was unaware that I
thought of applying for his release. He is one of
the very best and I feel ashamed that I may have
damaged his reputation in your eyes. We both
realise the importance of everyone doing and giving
their upmost in the next few months. My only
excuse is that I have just lost my husband and at
the time of writing you last I was feeling the loss
and loneliness and did not consider the
consequences to my son as I should. He is one of
the bravest and best so will you forget that I ever
asked for his release

Yours Faithfully
Mrs J. Hurt.

Flushed from meshed rust and ginger dead bracken and
bramble, a woodcock, russet-barred, uncalling,
swishes, explodes up, plumply zigzags.
      Underfoot: oval of steaming cupped stalks

faintly imprinted in frost-silvered leaf-mould, fecal sac
                                                still warm,
chestnut-edged buff wisp of down, $\left\{\begin{array}{l}\text{instants of tangible loss}\\ \text{instance}\end{array}\right.$

                    frail wisps bestraked like dead leaves

August 11th 1857

My dear Daughter,

I feel rather better this morning and am at Ashbourne Park. You may be sure I am wondering what you are all about this morning and what they are doing at Tonge without me. I am afraid the constant rain will injure the crops that are almost ripe for cutting. I have been writing a few lines —

The Trees in Ashbourne Park are Green
The Flowers are really Glowing —
But nothing like our own Sweet Rill
Forever ever flowing.

Thorpe Cloud may frown upon the Dove
Down at his foot low gliding
But Tonge's the Valley that I love
The place I would abide in.

None so sweet as the Valley of my own dear   [foxing and the fold of the paper render this paragraph illegible]

I wrote one half of this letter a day or two ago, but first one wants me & then another so I divide my time as well as I can amongst them all, and I am sorry to say Bessy Hurt is in a very poor way just now. She is 7 months gone in pregnancy, and often obliged to be in bed. It was her birthday on Sunday but she was forc'd to take her dinner in bed. We were all in Hurt's great room — we had a leg of Mutton & Caper sauce, a laid pudding & jellies and Plumb Cake at Tea, wine and biscuits after. I am glad to say she is rather better today. I am expecting to leave here every day now — so I shall call to stay at Derby if I am not sent for home. Write a little line to me my love. I feel nervous about them at home. Excuse me this time — I will write again soon — with love to dear John, I remain, my best beloved child,

Yr affectionate Mother.

Donnée of time and $\begin{cases} \text{topography} \\ \text{cartography} \end{cases}$ — *Ashes Valley at sunset:*
duck-egg gashed gold, splashed maroon; dulling to indigo
bruise.

1859 Plan of the Camberwell Cemetery, Forest Hill Road, S.E. Published by H. Cornford, Monumental Sculptor, Adjoining Entrance, Forest Hill Road, Peckham Rye. (Memorials of every description Restored and Renovated. Inscriptions Engraved. Imperishable Letters in Stone, Marble, or Granite. 30 Years Established. Illustrated Designs upon Application, or Free By Post. Special Fancies will be prepared when required.)

On verso, tremulous sepia holograph: *Grave this, ornate, in Granitt — "In Loving Memry of Thomas Ashbourne Hurt, Infant Son of Thomas and Elizabeth Hurt, Died March 11th, 1859, Aged 17 Months."*

10 years and 3 months old; on the paper-white
temple, a turquoise vein like a hieroglyph;
   Lucozade, crumbs of cake — each bird-sip
    after a minute is puked up, rancid;

flaxen hair shed in handfuls, her cranium
bald as a pawn (unkind chemotherapy).
   Medic and poetaster glibly
    (equally impotent platituders)

                    tender inadequate barbs.

Yesterday's lorry's blackstrap delivery –
(26 tonnes) the tanker bloke couldn't quite
　　get it all in; the pipes, uncoupled,
　　　　leaked a few gallons of glossy, thick gunge.

So, in the alley by the molasses tank,
next to the wheat and maize-gluten intake pit,
　　viscid morass of inch-deep treacle,
　　　　under a skin of chaff, oozes, sticky.

Recently fledged, three *Passer domesticus,*
lured by the grained crust, flounder in gluey drool,
　　primaries syruped, eyes sealed sweetly,
　　　　flap, flop amorphously, blackstrapped dumplings.

Three-fingered Fazzy, hard-case, the Grinderman,
gathers them gently into his denim bib,
　　nestles them fondly, runs warm water
　　　　into the millworkers' bog's cracked wash-bowl,

mumblingly croons as he cleanses the sweet down *Frail little*
　　　　　　　　　　　　　　　　　　　　　　poor things
　[*poor little frail little things; frail little poor little things*].

On the same front page: **ARABS IN A-BOMB BID/
NHS BOSS BACKS HIV VIRUS BLITZ**.
 From the Globe's fag-smoked beery parlour:
  …course it's the kiddies as I feels for like,

see worra means like, they Middle Easter lot,
them gets the hay bomb, that's like the hultimate,
 once them starts lobbin they fings round mate
  no fuckergonnerav no chance mister,

 them's got this Hallah (that's like the gord theym got),
them reckons all folks should ave this Hallah chap,
 that's why them ates they Jooz an that see,
  they Middle Easters'll start the Fird War,

same as they Haids as theym got in the *Sun* like, trouble o
                                        Haids is…
[Poor kids, twice-vulnerable: some other godly twits' war/

                        your own too-dangerous love.]

Tonge, March 12th, 1859.

My dear Emily,

It is my very painful task to tell you that your beloved sister Sophia Mary expired at 3 this morning after a very severe conflict with her last enemy Death — but she has done with all her sufferings now and entered on Glory everlasting. I am distressed beyond measure that it seems you are not in a fit state to come it has pleased the Almighty to take from us the best of Daughters and most caring of all sisters — cannot tell you what I passed through tell you how very distressed I am to let you know but if I did not I should be very uneasy I do not know what I am doing by letting you know — use all the fortitude you can and she is Happy and all is well — ah! frail poor little frail beings — Oh I have much to tell you — tell John she would be pleased I am sure if he could come and attend her remains to the Grave.

Emily I do not know how I write I have written to most of her cousins this morning God be with us I want some one to hold my distressed trembling heart this is the greatest sorrow I have ever felt — pray — pray for me — your Aunt is here and I have Jane Bonson but Oh! I have not my delight my Sophy Mary my Jesus has taken my beautiful blossom at 4 and twenty Oh my Saviour keep me in

the hollow of thine hand "I was not at rest, neither
was I in safety neither was I quiet yet trouble came"
Oh let us prepare for our last moments — that and
none other is the greatest wisdom

        I will not attempt to tell you my feelings for
it is in vain

    Come or send but you very like cannot come, as
from the nature of your dear sister's disease she cannot
be kept long I cannot act I am so very shattered with
musing and extream sorrow & grief, write to me and
I will answer it immediately Yr Loving much
distressed Mother.

Thirty years friendship, brief letters latterly,
mostly on matters ornithological,
    so it's an automatic mental
        tic to compose as I do this evening

Very good views of Buteo lagopus,
dark carpal patches, dark tips to primaries,
    terminal broad dark band to white tail -
        do you remember that one we saw in…?

then to recall that to do so is nuts. To you Marie, therefore,
    (since it's pathetic and mad to address oneself to the dead)

I re-address these notes on the raptor [even though, really,
    it's not yourself but your son with whom I still correspond].

Thick rhododendrons curtained the, even then,
mouldering disused outside proscenium,
crumbling dais backed by a stuccoed cowl
from which a player's lines would be ricocheted
into the bosky shades of a city park's
shrubby, neglected corner. A Lower IVth
strutted the wormed boards cockily *Out, out*ing,
callowly slighting time and Melpomene.

Urinous, burnt-out, relic of civic wealth
29 years on: wintery sun projects
(onto flaked stucco daubed with despair-runes) a
palimpsest walking shadow. A fingernail
rot-tests the wreckage, strays to a middle-aged
wattle of jowl-flab, substance of candle-wax.

My Dear,

I have been writing a few lines on poor Gipsy
Moses. Will you accept them?

Ye little birds on every bough
    Hush! while that dark eye closes
While the mist of death hangs on the brow
    Of sprightly Gipsy Moses.

Ye winds a solemn silence keep
    Stir not the wild hedge roses
Disturb ye not the last frail sleep
    Of dark-ey'd Gipsy Moses.

As some fair flower on Beauty's wreath
    Droops ere the sun light closes
So look'd he on his bed of death
    The lovely Gipsy Moses.

And Ah! his favourite violin
    Apollo thou shalt take it
For it would a be cruel sin
    For mortal hand to wake it,

And rather to the Ocean's brine
    Poor Mosey I would toss it
Than any other hand than thine
    Should draw the bow across it.

The dust lies on his coffin lid
    On him the green sward closes
But fairer flower earth never hid
    Than dark-ey'd Gipsy Moses.

Poor Moses is buried at Witwake near the Charn-
wood Forest. Old Dalleritha has been ill ever since he
died. You remember your dear sister Sophy Mary
sending him the arrow root and wine? — she would
not let Dalleritha take it in fear she should drink it
herself — you remember taking it to the tent [foxed
and faded beyond comprehensibility] for we bring our
years to an end like a tale that is told. Yr Loving
Mother.

Knobbled amorphous purple grotesqueries,
  tubers of malformed beetroot — the *saucisson*
    arthritic fingers of my father
      fumblingly clutch at a worn-smooth pawn skull,

counter, at least for a couple of moves, the
                                pressing advance of
  (tongue-lolling, wild-eyed) the crazed palfrey of
                          pale polished ash.

[Clearing the family's home for the next crowd's
                                    vacant possession:
long box of letters whose dead scribes correspond with us
                                                    still.]

Tonge, July 21st, 1862

It gives me joy in the midst of all my sorrows to know that you have made up your mind to come once more through much fatigue and anxiety to see your poor dear solitary Mother, a Mother that has been longing to see you for years — day and night sighing on account of your long absence, but thank God you have made up your mind to come to your dear old Home once more. God bless you, and bring you and your babies safe to me. I am but very poorly this morning. I am at Breedon & I have enquired about what John Roulstone will charge from Ashby for 3 of you — he will charge sixpence for you and threepence apiece for the children, and I think nothing at all for the Box if it is not very large, but never mind about that for you are sure to be met with some of us. Now remember, he will start from Edmond Leawood's at the Waggon & Horses in Church Street exactly at 5-o'clock in the afternoon — but you will be met, so do not make yourself in any way uneasy about that.

Give dear Heppy Joyce's love to her dear Brother Harry, and she is in full expectation of seeing you soon now. So write again and let me know if you shall come on next Saturday or the Saturday after. Be sure you tell me exactly that there may be no mistake. I am sure there are no complaints or fevers prevalent at this time, for which I am very thankful. Do not think of bringing much luggage as you will have enough to do to bring yourselves — and the worst dresses the dears have are better than Edwin's poor children have. I want nothing in this world but to see you and the dears — I hope you will give your heart to God, for without Him we can do nothing. Pray that he will take us all under the Shadow of his wings, there is no real safety elsewhere.

Give my love to John Shoebridge and thank him for letting you come. I should indeed be most happy to see him again down in Leicestershire — I hope he will come whilst I live to see him once more. Guide us Oh! Thou great Jehovah, we are weak and frail things but Thou art Mighty. Write directly on receipt of this — I hope you will soon behold old Breedon Church, and believe me your ever dear and affectionate Mother.

[…when they read this, it may be already done…]
Low over dim pines, dactylic phrases croak
    (*Scolopax rusticola* roding),
        finishing off in a sneeze-like high 'tswick',

[…supine in bracken…] the only other sound is a rattle
  (barbs in a brown plastic phial): — ◡ ◡ | — ◡ ◡ | —

SUPPLEMENTARY REPORT.

On the 1st. of March, 1945, Troop H.Q. and No. 2 Section accompanied Brigade H.Q., 45 (RM) Commando and No. 6 Commando on the Advance from AFFERDEN to WELL.

The main task allocated to the Troop was the opening of the rd from AFFERDEN (M/R: 395388, Eastern Holland 1/25,000 Sheet 4302) to BERGEN Cross-Roads (M/R: 831353, Eastern Holland 1/25,000 Sheet 4302). This rd had been extensively mined, cratered and blocked. For this Operation the Section were under Command 241 Fd Company. One D.6 Bulldozer and one D.4 Bulldozer were made available to the Section. This equipment proved of great value.

The rd was of good macadam construction and visual search for mines was possible. Clearance Parties checked the verges of the rd. Two other parties were employed in filling two large craters. These were filled by knocking down bombed houses with a Bulldozer and transporting the rubble to the craters by lorry and filling in. Subsequently the Bulldozers were used to remove such trees as could not be removed by hand from the rd. The enemy having retreated rapidly, the Section were able to make speedy progress and the BERGEN Cross-Roads were reccied at approximately 1500 hours.

Two large sized craters were found at this point surrounded by a barbed wire fence

with "MINEN" Signs attached. A suitable
divergence existed and it was decided
that it would be quicker to sweep the di-
vergence, which consisted of a rd surface,
than the crater itself. Two parties were
employed on this clearance and Schu mines
were discovered and lifted on the verge.
During this operation some type of Booby
Trap was initiated by the right hand
clearance party resulting in the death of
CH/X104783 Marine T BANCROFT and Po.X.
101922 (T) Mne (L/Cpl) B. HURT; Po.X.
116223 Marine W.G. PALMER being severely
wounded. Marine T. BANCROFT was thrown
some 30 feet from the site of the explosion
into the crater in the middle of the rd;
L/Cpl B. HURT was thrown some 60 ft into an
orchard adjoining the rd; Mne W.G. PALMER
was heard to cry for help and a party pro-
ceeded to probe their way towards him.
When they had reached the foot of the em-
bankment Lieut. J.J.A. MCLAREN appeared
on the scene in his Jeep and proceeded to
follow along the White Tape carrying First
Aid equipment. When Captain P.W.J. NEALE
was within a few feet of W.G. PALMER an
explosion occurred which had been caused
by Lieut. J.J.A. MCLAREN treading upon a
Schu mine. The clearing party were thrown
in various directions and minor injuries
caused to Capt A.B. JACKSON RM and Marine
G. DOWNING. Lieut J.J.A. MCLAREN was very
severely wounded in the legs. Capt P.W.J.
NEALE RM then directed further clearance
of Schu mines to enable Lieut J.J.A. MCLA-
REN and Marine W.G. PALMER to be removed
from the Minefield. Marine L.J. PRICE who
had been following the party laying the
Tape behaved with exemplary coolness de-

spite the fact that he had been in close proximity to both explosions and had suffered a cut in the face. The casualties were successfully removed from the Minefield and evacuated immediately by ambulance. The bodies of Marine T. BANCROFT and L/Cpl B. HURT were recovered by TSM D.J.R. MORSS RM and members of the Section and burial effected on the site; it was impossible to recover any documents.

A detailed report of this incident has been rendered to the Brigade Commander.

During the night Troop supplied Mine Clearance Party under Command Cpl J. MCCORKINDALE to 45 (RM) Commando who reccied a Route from BERGEN Cross-Roads to WELL. The remainder of the Section continued to maintain the AFFERDEN-BERGEN Cross Rds road and improve the causways made over the craters.

A Bailey Bridge at AFFERDEN was also maintained by the Section.

P. Fashpoint-Shellingem (Major RM)
O.C. No. 1 Troop, R.M. Engineer Commando.

Att HQ 1 Cdo Bde,
B.L.A.
5 Mar, 45.
PFS/FPC

But the *availability* of the things...
pox on all quacks who won't prescribe knock-out drops
(not with an irresponsible randomness,
   but with humane good grace to ~~those~~ glum
                    us
    terminals knowingly ready for it).

Fleet St conveys guerrilla activity
deep in Sri Lankan forest — a cyanide
   pellet depends from each one's necklace:
in the event of capture or overthrow...
    infinite luxury (7 seconds).

Briefly this *gravitas* weighting the conversation at breakfast
  lightens 'Gorillas, though, Dad, surely aren't clever enough?'

rustle of old gratuitous scrivenings

          frail wisps of dead bestraked leaves

          crackle of anhydrous bay

          — ∪ ∪ | — ∪ ∪ | —
          Croxley pa pyrus and bond

          ‖ — ∪ ∪ | — ∪ ∪ | —

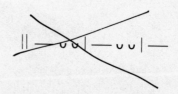